JB MOSES
Schaefer, A. R.
Grandma Moses /
Heinemann Library,c2003.
32 p. :ill. (some col.) ;

The Life
and Work
of...

Grandma Moses

Adam Schaefer

Heinemann Library
Chicago, Illinois

Design by Heinemann Library
Page layout by Jennifer Lee
Photo research by Alan Gottlieb
Printed and bound in China by Leo Paper Group.

07
10 9 8 7 6 5 4 3

Library of Congress Cataloging-in-Publication Data
Schaefer, A. R. (Adam Richard), 1976-
        Grandma Moses / Adam Schaefer.
          p. cm. -- (The life and work of--)
        Summary: Examines the life and work of the twentieth-century
        American painter, describing and presenting examples of her art.
        Includes bibliographical references and index.
        ISBN 978-1-4034-0289-9 (HC) ISBN 978-1-4034-0495-4 (Pbk)
        ISBN 1-40340-289-2 -- ISBN 1-40340-495-X (pbk.)
        1. Moses, Grandma, 1860-1961--Juvenile literature. 2.
        Painters--United States--Biography--Juvenile literature. [1. Moses,
        Grandma, 1860-1961. 2. Artists. 3. Art appreciation.] I. Title. II.Series.
        ND237.M78 S33 2003
        759.13--dc21   2002004020
        [B]   CIP

Acknowledgments
The publisher would like to thank the following for permission to reproduce photographs:

pp. 4, 5, 6, 7, 8, 9, 10, 11, 12, 13, 16, 17, 18, 20, 21, 22, 23, 25, 26, 27, 28 Grandma Moses Properties. Co., New York; p. 14 Hoosick Township Historical Society/ Louis Miller Museum; pp. 15, 24 Bettmann/Coribs; p. 19 Courtesy of the Hallmark Archives, Hallmark Cards, Inc.; p. 29 Lee Stalsworth/The National Museum of Women in the Arts

Cover photographs by Grandma Moses Properties Co., New York.

Special thanks to Katie Miller and to Jane Kallir and the staff at Grandma Moses Properties Co., New York, for their help in the preparation of this book.

Some words in this book are in bold, **like this.** You can find out what they mean by looking in the Glossary.

Contents

Who Was Grandma Moses?

Anna Mary Robertson Moses was an American painter. She is known by her **nickname,** Grandma Moses. Anna Mary never went to art school. She painted what she knew.

Haying Time, 1945

Anna Mary lived on a farm. She painted scenes of farms and small towns. Her art showed how people lived in the United States long ago.

Early Years

The Childhood Home of Anna Mary Robertson Moses, 1942

Anna Mary Robertson was born on September 7, 1860, in Greenwich, New York. She lived on a farm with her nine brothers and sisters. When she became an artist, Anna Mary painted this picture of the farm where she grew up.

Anna Mary helped her parents on the farm. When she was 12, Anna Mary went to another farm to help. She earned money that she brought home to share with her family.

Moving Away

Anna Mary worked for different families for 15 years. When she was 27, she married Thomas Salmon Moses. They moved to Virginia. They bought a farm, and started a family. This photograph shows Anna Mary with two of her children.

8

Black Horses, 1942

Anna Mary and Thomas had ten children.
Five of them died soon after they were born.
In 1905, when Anna Mary was 45, the family
bought a farm near Eagle Bridge, New York.
This painting shows the land around
Eagle Bridge.

Starting to Paint

English Cottage Flower Garden

Anna Mary and Thomas worked hard on the farm until Thomas died in 1927. Anna Mary was 67 years old. Her children had moved away, and she was lonely. She started to do **embroidery,** a way of making pictures using thread and cloth.

10

Autumn in the Berkshires

Sometimes her hands hurt when she did embroidery. A sister told Anna Mary that she should try painting. It would not hurt her hands, and she could still make art. Anna Mary started to paint in her spare time.

Showing Her Paintings

Anna Mary started painting **full-time** when she was in her 70s. She painted scenes from area farms and towns. Her friends and family told her that her paintings were good.

Bondsville Fair, 1945

Anna Mary decided that she would show her paintings in public. She showed her paintings at fairs near her home. People liked her paintings, but she did not win many prizes.

First Sale

In 1938, when Anna Mary was 77, a man from New York City saw her paintings in a store window. The man was an art collector named Louis Caldor. He liked Anna Mary's work, and bought the paintings for two dollars each.

He liked her paintings so much that he helped get her work in an **exhibition.** The exhibition was at a famous museum, the Museum of Modern Art, in New York City.

Some Shows in New York

Caldor introduced Anna Mary's work to Otto Kallir. Kallir was an owner of another gallery in New York City. Anna Mary had her first **solo exhibition** at Kallir's gallery in 1940.

The exhibition was called "What a Farmwife Painted." Some people from a big New York store saw the exhibit. They asked Anna Mary to show some of her paintings at the store's Thanksgiving Festival.

Reaching More People

New York **reporters** started to write about Anna Mary. They found out she had a large family. Her family and friends called Anna Mary "Grandma Moses." The newspapers started to call her that, too.

Hallmark Card with Grandma Moses Illustration

Anna Mary became famous. Her paintings were printed on cards. People liked sending Christmas cards with her art on them. Her paintings reminded people of what Christmas was like when they were children.

A Famous Artist

Anna Mary wrote a book about her life. Bookstores put the book in their windows. The book sold well. People wanted to learn about how a farmer became a famous painter.

The Eisenhower Farm, 1956

President Dwight D. Eisenhower liked Anna Mary's art, too. He had also lived on a farm. He asked Anna Mary to paint this picture of his farm. She went to meet the President and gave him the painting.

Painting History

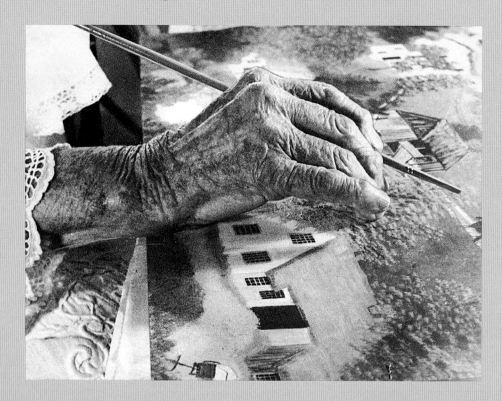

Anna Mary was a busy artist. She made more than 1,000 paintings in her lifetime. Her paintings showed how America changed over time. Sometimes she painted things from her childhood, like candle-making. Other times she painted newer things, like cars.

Anna Mary painted things from her **memory**.
She had an old table in her house where
she sat and painted every day. Sometimes
she would also go outside and paint the land
around her farm.

Making Money

Many artists do not make much money for their work during their lives. Anna Mary made a lot of money for her paintings. Companies gave her money so they could use her paintings on Christmas cards and fabric.

Thanksgiving Turkey, 1943

In 1950, Anna Mary was 90 years old. This
painting was given to a famous museum, the
Metropolitan Museum of Art, the same year.
Anna Mary was still selling paintings. She
became even more **popular**.

A Big Birthday Party

Anna Mary turned 100 years old on
September 7, 1960. She was on the cover
of magazines. The **governor** of New York
called the day "Grandma Moses Day."
People all over New York celebrated Anna
Mary's birthday.

26

Sugaring Off, 1960

People were amazed at Anna Mary's **talent,** age, and health. She was still living on her farm and painting. She painted this picture when she was more than 100 years old.

A Peaceful Ending

July Fourth

Anna Mary Robertson Moses died on December 13, 1961. She was more than 101 years old. For most of her life, Anna Mary was a farmer. But she is remembered as a famous artist. Many of her paintings are in museums. This one is in the White House, in Washington D.C.

Anna Mary's art tells what life used to be like in farms and small towns in America. Her paintings are still popular today. People all over the United States visit museums to look at her paintings.

Timeline

1860   Anna Mary Robertson is born, September 7.

1861-65 U.S. Civil War

1887   Anna Mary marries Thomas Moses and moves to
           Virginia.

1905   Anna Mary and her family move back to New York.

1914-18 World War I

1927   Thomas Moses dies.

1938   Louis Caldor buys Anna Mary's works.

           Anna Mary is included in a New York exhibition.

1940   Anna Mary has a solo exhibition in New York City.

1941-45 World War II

1940s   Anna Mary's paintings are on millions of Christmas
           cards.

1960   Anna Mary's 100th birthday is celebrated as
           "Grandma Moses Day."

1961   Anna Mary Robertson Moses dies, December 13.

Glossary

embroidery picture formed by pulling yarn or thread in different colors through cloth

exhibition show of works of art in public

full-time to do something as a job, every day

governor person who leads a state in the United States

memory things someone has learned or remembered and stored in the brain

nickname name that friends and family use for someone instead of the real name

popular liked by many people

reporter person who writes stories for a newspaper

solo something that is done by only one person

talent being able to do something better than other people

Index

More Books to Read

Nikola-Lisa, W. *The Year with Grandma Moses: Selected Writing and Paintings by Grandma Moses.* New York: Penguin Putnam Books for Young Readers, 2000.

More Artwork to See

Autumn. Bennington Museum. Bennington, Vermont.

The Old Hoosick Bridge. 1947. Strong Museum. Rochester, New York

A Fire in the Woods. 1947. National Gallery of Art. Washington, D.C.

Early Sugaring Off. 1944. The Gihon Foundation. Santa Fe, New Mexico.